REMEMBER, REMEMBER

Edited by

Sarah Marshall

First published in Great Britain in 2004 by
ANCHOR BOOKS
Remus House,
Coltsfoot Drive,
Peterborough, PE2 9JX
Telephone (01733) 898102

All Rights Reserved

Copyright Contributors 2004

SB ISBN 1 84418 310 6

FOREWORD

Anchor Books is a small press, established in 1992, with the aim of promoting readable poetry to as wide an audience as possible.

We hope to establish an outlet for writers of poetry who may have struggled to see their work in print.

The poems presented here have been selected from many entries, and as always editing proved to be a difficult task.

I trust this selection will delight and please the authors and all those who enjoy reading poetry.

Sarah Marshall
Editor

CONTENTS

Bonfire Night	Jean P McGovern	1
Gunpowder, Treason And Plot, And Why Not?	Ben E Corado	2
The Anonymous Girl	Samantha Lomax	4
Catherine Wheel	Tony Bush	5
Guy Fawkes - Bonfire Night	C Gascoigne	6
The Wonders Of Guy Fawkes Night	Robert D Hayward	7
Bonfire Night	Ann Voaden	8
Bangs And Crashes	Margaret Marston	9
Ode To A Bap	Christopher Head	10
The Bonfire	Frank Tonner	11
Excitement, Delightment, It's Bonfire Night	Jennifer Austin	12
Bangers And Sparklers	Michael Fenton	13
Bonfire Night	June Melbourn	14
Bonfire Night	D Marc Rogers	15
The Truth About Guy Fawkes Night	Nicolette Turner	16
A Guy's Lament	Desmond Quick	17
Bonfire Night	Catrina Lawrence	18
Fireworks	Anne Davey	19
Bonfire Night	Gary Raymond	20
Do We Really Need To?	Gillian Mullett	21
Remember, Remember	Norman Bissett	22
Bonfire Poem	Dai Blatchford	23
Remember, Remember	Brian Ducker	24
Writing, The Bonfire Poem	Stanley Bruce	25
Bonfire Night	Karen Hodgetts	26
Why Is It?	Julia L Holden	27
He's The Tops	Jon EL Wright	28
Thoughts On November 5th	S J Dodwell	29
Smoke Signals	F A C	30
The Bonfire	A V Carlin	31
Remember, Remember The 5th November	Letitia Snow	32

Title	Author	Page
Death Row Scarecrow	Vann Scytere	34
Remember, Remember	Jean Kelly	35
Ode To Passion	Denise Delaney	36
The Big Bang	Chris Needley	37
Bonfire	Mia Clarke-Edden	38
Bonfire Night	Frances Dyke	39
Childhood Bonfire Night	Charlotte Clare	40
Of No Colour	Michael D Bedford	41
If Only	Gloria thorne	42
The Great Bonfire Collecting Ritual	Jonathan Pegg	43
Bonfire Night	Rosemary Davies	44
November Fifth	Margery Rayson	45
All Because Of Guy Fawkes	Janet Collinson	46
Guy Fawkes	Mary Hodges	47
Bonfire Night	Janet M Baird	48
Firework Night	Jo Lodge	49
Guy Fawkes Night	Mollie D Earl	50
The Fifth Of November	Rachel Mary Mills	51
Bonfire Burning	Heather Denham	52
Bonfire Night	Maggie Strong	53
Bonfire Night	Hardeep	54
Bonfire Night	Janet Cavill	55
The Time Of Year Again!	Rowland Patrick Scannell	56
The 5th Of November	Maureen Sponar	57
Magical Lights	Rose Murdoch	58
Remember, Remember	Sarah Blackmore	59
Remember, Remember	R Wiltshire	60
Figure On The Fire	M C Jones	62
Guy Fawkes	S L Groves	63
Rockets, Smoke And Glitter	Carol Ann Darling	64
Masters Of The Sky	Guy Fletcher	66
Surplus	Simon Daniels	67
A Real Bonfire	Maureen Westwood O'Hara	68
November 5th	Pat Heppel	69
Bonfire Night Sonnet	Mick Nash	70
November	Joy Morton	71
Jubilee Bonfire	Christopher T Coney	72

Title	Author	Page
Bonfire Night	E M Eagle	73
Bonfire Night Memories Revisited	D I Muncaster	74
Bonfire Night	Anne Lawry	75
Bonfire Night Fireworks	Violetta J Ferguson	76
Moments Of Light	Carole A Cleverdon	77
Gunpowder Plot	James Stephen Cameron	78
Guy Fawkes Night	Therese G Gilbert	80
The Firework Party	Robert Allen	81
Remember The 5th Of November	Lynne Cassels	82
Bonfire	Lucy May Harrison	83
Bonfire Night	Holly Laisby & Beth Pedley	84
Bonfire Night	Rebecca Smith & Lucy Harrison	85
Firework Nights	Rowene	86
Fireworks - Two Views	Joan Howlett	87
Fireworks On The Fifth	Ruth Daviat	88
Enlightening	Mark Redfern	89
Gunpowder Treason	Kathy Rawstron	90
November Fifth	P S D MacArthur	92
Bonfire Night - Past And Present Memories	Janet Ramsden	93
Pleased To Remember The Fifth Of November	Enid Thomas	94
Bonfire Night	B J Green	95
Though November Skies Are Sometimes Red And Glowing . . .	Jackie J Docherty	96
Embers Of The Past	Robin Halder	98
Bonfire Night	Ramandeep Kaur	99
Autumn Magic	Gwen Hoskins	100
Autumn . . . Is It Good Or Bad?	Mrinalini Dey	101
Fireworks	David Sheasby	102

BONFIRE NIGHT

Fireworks night can be a lovely display
When it's worked out, in a particular way
As people stand around, watching the bonfire aglow
While fireworks explode, making a lovely show

With jacket potatoes, making quite a picnic
With goodies we like to choose, and pick
While, colourful fireworks fly through the air
For all that surrounds it, and for all to share

When we celebrate the 5th of November
It's a traditional night, for us to remember
Through the history of Guy Fawkes, burnt at the stake
As we listen to yellow-orange crackles of wood, as we break

When fireworks are exploded, well before time
Why not keep bonfire night a special, colourful sign
Especially when fireworks go whizzing, through the sky
A month before time, leaving the elderly in despair and to sigh

A firework display is beautiful, on a special occasion
When we make up a dummy, with very old clothing
Keeping ourselves warm, with lots to eat
Feeling contented, with this traditional treat

So as we look up in awe, at the colourful display
Guy Fawkes is paraded, then burnt to this day
So do we really understand, what does it mean?
A republican, a Catholic, fighting for freedom, a Gaelic dream.

Jean P McGovern

Gunpowder, Treason And Plot, And Why Not?

I know it's almost four hundred years ago but we were still around in those days,
We didn't suddenly appear outside football stadiums or car boot sales in the seventies,
Yes, us chuck wagon chefs were around many centuries before then,
But not in the same form as we have today, selling burgers, kebabs and cans of Coca-Cola,
From a mobile home on wheels with a paraffin lamp for heat on a cold winter's evening.
No, back in 1605, chuck wagons were a little more basic as we sold from a wooden cart,
Which we lit a fire beside and chucked a pig's ear on the spit as requested,
There were no microwave ovens in those distant and dark years of James I.

Anyway, I was selling my meat on the banks of the smelly olde River Thames,
When I noticed a muffled commotion coming from the Houses of Parliament,
Out of the flames of my fire, I could spot a few gentlemen pushing barrels into a tunnel,
I thought nothing peculiar of the incident and carried on serving leg of wild boar,
It had been a busy evening, as there had been a public hanging only an hour previously,
You are always guaranteed a crowd after such entertainment, people tend to get hungry.

After I'd sold the last of my slabs of meat, I shut up my wooden cart for the night,
I made myself a torch and decided to investigate what was going on,
There was a young boy of about twelve, pushing more and more barrels into that tunnel.

'Is that enough, Mr Fawkes?' he cried. He told me there were over two hundred down there,
Soon as the leaders of the plot appeared out of the tunnel, the young child said to me,
'Hey Mister, give us your torch, we're going to blow that ugly building to smithereens,'
I was quite happy to assist, especially as I knew James 1 was also inside having a coffee,
I'd hated him ever since he bought a pig's trotter, chewed it and then spat it out in front of me.

Just as I was about to hand it over, the King's henchmen grabbed my shoulder,
I was swiftly arrested, along with the boy, a dozen other perpetrators and Guy Fawkes himself,
Immediately sentence was passed and in the morning, we'd be hung from the gallows,
Word had spread like wildfire through London and a crowd of thousands had turned up,
They supported everything Guy Fawkes had done to assassinate the tyrant James 1,
Overnight he had become a martyr, probably the first icon that this country ever had.

As I stood there on the gallows awaiting execution, I noticed thousands of people had painted,
The face of Guy Fawkes on their coats. He truly had become a martyr for the people.

Ben E Corado

The Anonymous Girl

I used to jewel the night with my name
Safe beneath layers of knitted love
With treacle toffee to clag my tongue
And the moon pouring cream down from above

Dad would whoosh a Catherine wheel
While Mum marked the hot potato dance
To the shimmering fizz of fountain sparks
And mugs of soup between gloved hands

But now the night is scarred with fear
As I scarf behind my locks and doors
Mum and Dad have long fizzled out
The memories are scabbed-over sore

The coal sky drips its diamonds still
But my name stays mute within my heart
For the ones that laughed and ran away
Having thrown and burnt my life apart.

Samantha Lomax

CATHERINE WHEEL

Kate.
Catherine Wheel.

Left only char-mark traces on
this dirty laundry line post:
unrequited love so brightly shone
scarred by a pyrotechnical ghost.

Spun.
Vibrant fire.

White-hot with turquoise-spangled eyes,
burnt, exploded, rattled death;
as tails of auburn fireflies
blew kisses of fleeting gossamer breath.

Flash.
Sudden dark.

Spectral afterburn, protoplasmic and cold
then nothing save a vacant space
dreams and youth fell numb and old
in the vacuum of lost embrace.

Kate.
Catherine Wheel.

Spent firework, beckons yet she warns
burnt offerings are the end of it;
a heart may ache and forever mourn,
some things should never be re-lit.

Tony Bush

GUY FAWKES - BONFIRE NIGHT

Those flashing lights, those glittering stars
Way up in the November sky,
Such brilliance, such beauty, is brought to the human eye.
Young and old with thoughts untold all passing through the mind,
Good or bad, happy or sad, can be explained with a heartfelt sigh.
'I love to see the fireworks,' the little boy exclaimed,
'And hear that pop, pop, banging, with that magic coloured rain.'
That story which my daddy read, last night before I went to bed,
It told about a man, Guy Fawkes, who had some very evil thoughts.
'Here was a man,' my daddy said, 'who when good people were in bed
Did plan a dastardly deed. So up to London town he went,
Where destruction was his main intent.
He tried to blow up London town and bring the parliament
                                                  buildings down.
But no, the policemen of the day caught him and put him safe away,
Into the cells of London Tower, where he could spend his final hours
His final hour dwelling on his nefarious deeds.'
So now on the fifth of November, we remember
Gunpowder, treason and plot,
When Guy Fawkes thought he had a very good reason,
But then it got a little too hot.

C Gascoigne

THE WONDERS OF GUY FAWKES NIGHT

The glories of that autumn night -
When children's faces, young and bright,
Gaze up into a starlit sky
At golden fountains soaring high -
Are handed down from age to age
As history turns another page.

Crimson rockets rain down their showers,
Blossoming into choicest flowers;
Crackers jump head over heels,
While whirligigs and wooden wheels
Spin a dozen times a second -
Faster than Dad ever reckoned.

Purples, violets, silvers, golds,
Explode amongst Aurora's folds;
Fountain nymphs in precious bloom
Dance upon lawns, dispelling gloom;
And, shooting high, fire-breathing dragons
Ride upon their gilded wagons.

'To the bonfire!' people cry,
And gather round with sparklers. Why?
To boast the failure of the plot
To blow up Parliament - that pot
Of murder cooked by one Guy Fawkes
With gunpowder and secret talks.

That is, if people really know
Their history; if it's just a show,
We miss the point. Let's take this chance
To teach the world a different dance:
Let violence and conflict cease;
Let's celebrate - and share - Christ's peace.

Robert D Hayward

BONFIRE NIGHT

*Snap! Crackle! Bang! a*nd *Whizz!*
Colours sparkle, amaze,
as fireworks of intriguing style
dazzle the eyes above the blaze.
Wrapped in mufflers, gloves and hats,
many ages meet
to admire eccentricities
whilst stamping tired, cold feet.

Roman candles, rockets galore,
frothy silver fountain,
all effervesce in the darkling night
like Etna's bursting mountain.
Chinese lanterns a-whirling
excite the crowd whose shouts of glee
increase at the climax unfurling.

Crackle! Snap! and flames shoot high
as the bonfire, fully firing,
shows Guy Fawkes imagery
to watchers now slowly tiring.
Then armed with hot dogs from a stand,
footsteps reluctant and slow,
a quick last 'Ooh!' at the finale,
then it's surely time to go.

Crackle! Fizz! a belated *pop!*
The fire in embers now;
murmuring voices call goodnight,
too tired to make a row.
November Fifth once more is done,
fireworks cindered and spent;
fun was had by one and all
at the bonfire show to which they went.

Ann Voaden

BANGS AND CRASHES

Skies filled with flashes of light
Blue and red and green and white
Bangs and crashes all around
Explosions are the only sound

Bonfires blazing, crackling and hot
Potatoes and hot dogs, lots and lots
Sparklers flickering in tiny hands
Waving about like fiery wands

Guy Fawkes burning on the fire up there
People - they just stand and stare
Toffee apples and punch to drink
Makes it really hard to think

This is the tradition of this land
Guy Fawkes had ideas so grand
Wanted to destroy our parliament
So on the rack he suffered - without repent

Others too were in this plot
The death penalty is what they got
In the history books we read
Of the plotters and their deeds.

Margaret Marston

ODE TO A BAP

Who'd want to be a buttie?
Who'd want to be a bap?
Who'd want to be a wholegrain roll?
Born just to fill a gap!

The life is very short,
It's not a happy trend;
There's not even any time
To make a special friend!

You might greet a Baby Egg,
Mr Burger, Master Lamb,
Miss Fresh Lettuce, Ruddy Radish,
Or even Porky Ham!

Perhaps you'll meet Big Chippy,
Or that corny Mr Beef,
But sad to say, you've got no chance,
You'll end up 'twixt some teeth!

You're just an upside-down bap,
Whatever filling you have got.
Your top is on your bottom,
And your bottom's on your top!

Of course we know the answer:
A bap has got no soul.
That's why folk are lining up
To have another roll.

Christopher Head

THE BONFIRE

It's bonfire night,
Soon it will be set alight
Fireworks will light up the sky
I hope nothing goes awry.
Mums and dads dig deep into their pockets
So their children will have bangers and rockets,
Everyone standing round the fire
Watching the flames get higher and higher.
All too soon its dying embers
Will be all that the people remember.
I hope no one has been in fear
Because it's over now until next year.

Frank Tonner

EXCITEMENT, DELIGHTMENT, IT'S BONFIRE NIGHT

Roman candles and bangers, and rockets and sparklers,
Catherine wheels that spin bright through the darkness,
Flames dancing round,
To the crackling sounds,
Excitement, delightment, it's bonfire night.

Burning wood warms our hands on the cold, foggy night,
Blazing colours fill dark skies with vibrant light.
Popcorn and toffee,
A warm cup of coffee,
Excitement, delightment, it's bonfire night.

Hot baked potatoes and toasted marshmallows,
Leaping flames of burnt red, scorched orange and yellows,
A guy for the top,
With a whizz, bang and pop,
Excitement, delightment, it's bonfire night.

Jennifer Austin

BANGERS AND SPARKLERS

'Fires of bones and celebrations
of unexploded Parliaments, where
the babble continues even in
today's questionable recommendations.'

Remember the fifth of Novembers
as they come with Guy Fawkes' intent
to blaze the fires, to end in embers.
Releasing ancient anger into a grand event.

Let's never forget what those fires represent:
good firelight to warm November nights,
not bringing the fear of winter, but of thrill
to dance with Pagan vigour of delights,
circling the fires, having our fill
of ale and ginger beer, bangers and beans.

So drum the drums at a very fast beat,
up like rockets and down like sticks,
with wheels and squeals, bangs and scenes
of laughter and wonder, beating a retreat
from fireworks and bonfires in conga-style
making these happenings memorable high jinks
and so to bed with the reward of a smile.

Michael Fenton

BONFIRE NIGHT

It's bonfire night, so wrap up warm,
It's cold enough for snow,
The bonfire's lit upon the field,
It gives a cosy glow.

The children are holding sparklers,
They make a figure eight,
Some are eating hot dogs,
Or hot potatoes on a plate.

The rockets are whizzing up to the sky,
There's a bang, and colours galore,
Bright red and green and purple,
The crowd all shout for more.

Catherine wheels are spinning round,
Roman candles and fountains of rain,
It's a really enjoyable evening,
Another year till we do it again.

June Melbourn

BONFIRE NIGHT

On bonfire night I hear the sounds
Of crackling, creaking fire;
And see the 'Jackie Jumpers' bounds,
And see the mighty pyre.
Is this what happened long ago?
No. But could it though?

On bonfire night I see the sight
Of colours bursting on the night.
Lighting up the darkness,
Stars descend towards us.
Is this what happened long ago?
No. But could it though?

The burning of the arsonists
That reaches up to the sky,
The rolling cloud of smoke that mists
The real stars on high.
Is this what happened long ago?
No. But could it though?

Should we remember and recall?
We know *now* men will give their all
For their religion's sake.
God knows, 'tis a mistake.
This is what happened long ago.
Yes. But should it though?

D Marc Rogers

THE TRUTH ABOUT GUY FAWKES NIGHT

The truth about Guy Fawkes night
It was all a big mistake
Guy never meant to make a bomb
He meant to make a cake
You see guy was not political
He was a cook's assistant
He only posed a threat to those
Whose stomachs weren't resistant.
Whilst dreaming of his love one day
The cake mix he was making
Got mixed up with the gunshot from
The pheasant he was baking
The cake was fine until it rose
And then it rose some more
And then it blew the ceiling off
So that it was a floor
Two floors above the kitchen
Sat the unprepared PM
As a turbo-charged Dundee cake
Sent him hurtling on his BM.
The cake passed by the House of Lords
Whilst reaching for the sky
It gazed upon the sleeping peers
Then blew them all sky high
And though poor Guy got all the blame
And he went down in history
The plot of treason was to him
A complete and utter mystery.

Nicolette Turner

A Guy's Lament

The scruffy urchin on the street
Besought each passer-by,
In tones that now seem indiscreet,
A penny for the Guy.

On Guy Fawkes night the sky was bright,
Swift rocket rails amaze,
And Mum and Dad, with kids well clad,
Stood round the bonfire's blaze.

But time moves on, the Guy is gone
And children trick or treat,
Explosions sound from all around
In every town and street.

The battles rage day after day
At all hours, never ends;
We know full well it is sheer hell
For canine, feline friends.

I wonder what we celebrate
In competitions strife -
The affluence or effluence
Of modern spendthrift life?

One hundred pounds go up in smoke
For self-indulgent treats,
And homeless generations
Sleep in boxes on the streets.

We could have fed the hungry
Or done battle with disease,
Could we retry the Penny Guy
I ask you
Could we
Please!

Desmond Quick

BONFIRE NIGHT

The fifth of November,
Celebrations go wild,
Guy Fawkes burn,
Fireworks fly.

The fifth of November
Celebrations to wild,
Children cheer,
At all the big bangs.

The fifth of November,
Celebrations go wild,
Children run in streets
Shouting, 'A penny for the Guy.'

The fifth of November,
Celebrations go wild,
Cats and dogs run and hide,
As fireworks light the sky.

The fifth of November,
Celebrations go wild,
Parents watch with glee
As Guy Fawkes is destroyed.

Catrina Lawrence

FIREWORKS

Why do we let fireworks go on?
Yes, all of us know this is so wrong
Before and after people in pain, and in our hospitals they lay
Is it always going to be this way?
Knowing it's up to all of us
We won't only be making a fuss
Something has to be done
It isn't a matter that we have won
Safeguard our elderly and our kids
Now's the time to put on the lid
Let's stop all this harm and fear
Don't let it go on for another year
It's got to stop now.

Anne Davey

BONFIRE NIGHT

Fireworks fly high into the jet-black sky at night,
Exploding with a crackle, causing children to jump with delight,
Fireworks fall through the night like a meteor shower of raindrops,
Sprinkling to the ground, finally the colourful shower stops.
While the air smokes and as smell of powder clears,
One by one everybody goes home, full of bonfire night cheer.

Gary Raymond

Do We Really Need To?

Why must we keep remembering
Those who plotted the death of a king?
Is there nothing we have learnt?
When we see a euphony burnt
Treacherous men were on his side
When gunpowder Guy tried to hide
So this deed did not take place
An informant made great haste
To save his neck he made sure
And gave the plot away and more
So what do we celebrate?
Is it love or is it hate?
And why must we still endure
Noise and smoke, no one is sure
The mindless and the cruel it seems
Take no heed that it's obscene
To terrorise the old and weak
And animals that cannot speak
Is it time that Parliament
Give us peace and not relent
To have fireworks just once a year
And not for weeks that some now fear.

Gillian Mullett

REMEMBER, REMEMBER

Surely it's time to forget? To put the genie
back into the bottle and cork it?
For the Irish and Scots to stop re-enacting
400-year-old history and to declare
no contest over the Battle of the Boyne?

Personally, I have nothing against Guy Fawkes
and his sad gaggle of co-conspirators: Catesby,
Keyes, Winter, Rookwood, both the Percys,
Digby, Grant, Bates, Tresham, both the Wrights,
(and two Wrights don't necessarily make a wrong) -

that pathetic bunch of no-hopers. Losers. Imagine!
Hiring a cellar beneath the House of Lords!
Then, secretly (!) stashing away their 36 barrels of TNT,
their stack of faggots and cartload of firelighters,
their six month's supply of the Catholic Herald. Imagine!

The Centre for Explosion Studies, University of Wales
at Aberystwyth has usefully computed that that little lot,
if detonated, would have demolished Westminster Palace,
Big Ben, the Odeon, Leicester Square and Wembley Stadium,
although the Turner Prize for 1605 would not have been affected.

It was all such a long time ago.
Today's pyrolater's may well have forgotten the misty origins,
the dismal details - that is, if they ever knew.
They are accustomed, every evening, on the TV news,
to bigger and better bangs from hi-tech terrorist atrocities.

Personally, I have nothing against Guy Fawkes,
or Catholics in general. Indeed, some of my best friends . . .
Surely there are more appropriate modern monsters to stick on top
of our bonfires? If we must have bonfires,
let's have them on May 1st. Let's celebrate the beltane-spring.

Norman Bissett

BONFIRE POEM

Often I feel like a guest
at a bonfire party
wearing a clean white shirt
desperately affecting nonchalance
as the ketchup starts to squirt . . .

Dai Blatchford

Remember, Remember

I watch the bonfire from a distance now
I never join in the crowd
I see all the happy children
And I hear their laughter loud.

I can still smell the tangy wood smoke
And feel the magic of that place,
I can taste the half-roasted potatoes
And see the black smudges on my face.

It's a place I'll always remember
Bonfire night is so special to see,
It's there I chased my first girlfriend,
She's standing here now with me.

We have seen many bonfires together,
We have lit fireworks by the score,
Now we watch our children's children
Doing what we have done before.

We love the crackle and thunder
As rockets climb into the dark,
The squeeze of a hand as we remember,
Then a walk back home from the park . . .

Brian Ducker

WRITING THE BONFIRE POEM

It's bonfire night and I need
some words to inspire,
my young lad says,
'Well it's a big fire.'

To complete this poem,
I need more than that!
'Ah,' he says,
'Keep in the cat.'

Keep in your pets,
that's quite right,
you've got to remember that
on bonfire night.

'What about the fireworks?'
I say to my young lad.
'Fireworks and sparklers
are magic, Dad.'

'Anything else my boy,
that we can say?'
'Keep back from the bonfire and
the fireworks today.'

So I've written a poem,
that my boy has inspired,
he's quite a wee character,
but now he's getting quite tired.

So he's off to bed.
'Goodnight Dad, I had lots of fun,
I can't wait until tomorrow,
can we write another one?'

Stanley Bruce

BONFIRE NIGHT

On November the 5th on bonfire night
My evening is filled with fear and fright
As a cat, this month is a nightmare for me
All the flashes and bangs that I hear and see
Whistling and banging and whizzing all night
Scared and afraid, I shut my eyes tight
No way to escape or block out the sound
Except curling up tight in a dark corner I've found
Under the bed or behind the settee
Bonfire night is a nightmare for me.

Karen Hodgetts

WHY IS IT?

As Christians, that we
Claim to be, we still remember
The 5th of November, gunpowder,
Treason and plot we celebrate
With great glee, the fate of a man
Being tortured, hung, drawn and quartered.

Why is it that we claim to be
Concerned about pollution of the
Environment, and then burn anything
From old, smelly socks to granny's chair
On bonfires and so make November,
The month of fog to make
Us all cough and wheeze?

Why is it we profess to care for all
Creatures great and small, and
Show no concern when big bangs
And flashes go off all over the place,
Making the animal kingdom
Shake with terror?

Why is it that we don't
Think again and celebrate
Just a joyful, happy thing,
With a proper grand display,
When no child will get burnt?

Julia L Holden

HE'S THE TOPS

See the guy upon the fire
Massive rockets rising higher
All those bangs that emanate
Fulfilled wonder until late
In the darkness abound
'Trick or treat' we hear the sound
When enjoyed they are not bad
Except for peaking, shrieking *Dad!*

Jon EL Wright

THOUGHTS ON NOVEMBER 5TH

Fireworks, this year, are louder, brighter, more fun,
Lighting up the night like a nocturnal sun.
Flowering, sparkling, painting the sky
With patterns, colours, shapes right up high.

Bonfires glow deeply both yellow and red,
Wood crackles and snaps to form a stormy bed
For the ill-fated Guy Fawkes sitting there,
Consumed by dancing flames leaping in the air.

And when all is quiet and dark again,
Does anyone think of the hurt and pain
Caused by real guns with their noise and flashes,
The horrors of war reducing life to ashes?

S J Dodwell

Smoke Signals

Breathe it in, go on I dare you,
the wood-scent smoke from a glowing fire!
Raucous winds and scudding clouds
out with the brollies, on with the scarves.
Then from nowhere the sun appears,
summer's ghost shimmering down.
we peel our clothes, full stretch out and gently doze
tantalising wind: faint tinged by winter
chills prone body in warning 'counter,
taunting us from sweet repose.

Dark-drawn nights and short-lived days
the elements noisy and untamed
suited for All Hallows Eve
or Hallowe'en, followed by
All Saints, come Christians dream.
Prepare yourselves and cleanse the spirit,
ghosties, witches, be gone this minute!
By night again big bonfires blaze
wicked flames lick Guy Fawkes' knees,
crack, bang, whoosh, fireworks at large,
dazzling diamonds, opals, shooting stars.
Black nights and drab days moulder on
'til chanted on iced air from town to home,
'God rest you merry gentlemen!'

F A C

THE BONFIRE

On the fifth of November we celebrate bonfire night
And soon the big bonfire is well alight
The children gather around as the bonfire does glow
And the fireworks explode to make a colourful show.

And soon the flames of the bonfire light up the night sky
As they leap and dance around the feet of the guy
Perched right at the top of the huge bonfire
Soon the whole guy will be engulfed as the flames grow higher.

Yes the children love the excitement of bonfire night
The looks on their faces are a sheer delight
They shriek with laughter and excitedly shout
And now it is time to bring the toffee apples out.

A V Carlin

Remember, Remember The 5th November

In the year of our Lord sixteen hundred and five
When you were just thankful to still be alive
To bring up your family and live without fear
Guy Fawkes had ideas no one wanted to hear.

He was a Catholic, though that is no crime
But some people thought different in that faraway time
He decided the best way to make people heed
Was to devise a plan with a devilish deed.

He did not like the king who was then James the First
He thought to be ruled by him was a curse
So he rallied his friends and put forth his plan
To which they agreed to every last man.

They would hide under the Houses of Parliament
To blow the place up was their evil intent
So off they did go laden down with their gunpowder
To wait until what they thought was the right hour.

Always in secret they had met in the night
Thinking that no one would have them in sight
But the plot was discovered and they were caught
At least in our history that is what we are taught.

They paid for their crimes forfeiting their lives
And still to this day Parliament survives
Was he a martyr or traitor you ask
To even think of doing this terrible task?

You must make up your own mind but before you do
Celebrations of Guy Fawkes must come into view
On November the fifth with bonfires alight
Effigies of this man then come into sight.

The fireworks are lit to remember the plot
Think also of the penalty these people got
For the crime they committed so long ago
When they were hanged, where in *hell* did they go!

Letitia Snow

DEATH ROW SCARECROW

Darkness grew in a November
sky and flowers popped up
from a firework garden.
Only for a split second
of booming existence they
bloomed. Too quick to
gather and fill a vase with.
Coming from a secret
border planted by a phantom
in no particular order
grabbing our intention,
by brightness of invention.
These tall poppies became
the target of a marksman,
a sniper that never missed.
His shots rang out exploding
every flower head in
electric glow like coloured
drops of snow. All night
long they sang their song loud
and clear for everyone to
hear. Till exhaustion of
ammunition the bonfire's ash
petition a charcoal signature,
evidential DNA of our night's play.
Cold cloths burned, religion
spurned the morning mourned no
sense dawned. We couldn't wait
to do it all gain and plant those
seeds of man's misdeeds,
woeful weeds.

Vann Scytere

REMEMBER, REMEMBER

Potatoes, parkin, treacle toffee,
All washed down with scalding coffee.
Rosy cheeks, excitement showing,
As the flames are quickly growing.

Upturned faces towards the sky,
'Midst the chants of, 'Burn the guy.'
Spectacular colours, whistles, bangs,
Anticipation when darkness hangs.

Tradition! Madness rules again,
Legacy from a distant reign.
This, an arsonist's delight,
Of course I speak of bonfire night.

Charcoaled hedgehogs, terrified pets,
How much worse this madness gets.
Children, burned, scarred and maimed,
By forces which just won't be tamed.

How many horrors will we allow,
For a few short hours of pleasure now?
Question: Are you a Guy Fawkes fan,
Or should there be a total ban?

Jean Kelly

ODE TO PASSION

Caught by the abandoned beauty in the mourner's wail and weep,
Purity of emotion, innocent, broken, fresh and loud.
Sweet fear, desperation, frenzied rapture of given grief,
Remembered passion through carnal hysterics in the bonfire's crowd.
Empty chairs at a table, walls hollow, paradox gone, night looms,
No jaws to howl, dead without feeling, in bare and empty rooms.

Concealed mystery of man, to open the soul and laugh and moan,
Not only ecstasy of desperation, frailty in pain and loss we all
                                      embrace and own.
Details irrelevant to the swelling of the heart in ambivalence, fear
                                      or pain,
Relive past emotions well to ensure profundity not revealed in vain.
Passion lives on in the bonfire glow and the firework adrenaline squeal,
Although streamed out through laughter, still beauty, humbling
                                      and real.

Overwhelming to the psyche, outward signs of pain,
Yet the source of instinct sees fingerprints in the dancing of the flame,
Imagine the static in the air on that day of loss and shame.
Sweat, blood and tears.

Remember the fifth of November not for rhymed triviality,
Take away the fear on the streets, the desperate willingness to die,
It disrespects those who felt the air and corrupts the true humanity,
Turning souls into stereotypes makes all men gone a lie.
To understand the past, remember the reasons why and positively cope,
Fill the next generation with logic, laughter and love, to detour our
                                      repressive slope.

Remember, remember the fifth of November, blood, seat and tears,
The static lives on, in the fire, dance and song, that're let loose
                                      every year.

Denise Delaney

THE BIG BANG

I'm not very handsome nor very cute
In fact, I'm known more for being a brute
It's hard for someone like me
Who firmly believed that some things should not be
Why all the fuss about my belief
I thought it would bring some relief
They sit and spin all they can
I shudder to think what they would plan
As far as I'm concerned it had to stop
The lies, the banter, the whole lot
It's so very obvious and plain to see
Why I schemed and plotted what was to be
The plot was foiled and disallowed
Cos, someone went and split on my crowd
It infuriates me when I look back
Things should have been different after the attack
All I can do now is look back and sigh
Can you guess who I am?
'Yes, it's me, it's *Guy.*'

Chris Needley

BONFIRE
*(This poem is the result of studying
S Beckett's play 'End Game')*

We	
build	
and	debris
stack	thrownaway
skywards	year's
remnants	next
of	rebuild
a	to
year's	have
thrownaway	now
debris	We

Mia Clarke-Edden

BONFIRE NIGHT

Bonfire Night is not alright
Bang! Bang! Night after night
No peace. No rest for pets
Running scared we can see the hurts
The babies cry, I really wonder why
Mothers hold babies comforting try
To settle babies in their cots
Then there's poor old pussy cat
Up the trees they try to flee
Chooks on the farm and sheep agree
Elderly people, old people, think of war
As loud bangs shake the floor
Why should we celebrate Guy Fawkes
It's not something good but devil's works

Frances Dyke

Childhood Bonfire Night

It had to be before the war of course -
We could not light the sky for alien force,
But in those far-off days we dared be bright
And make a splendid fire for Guy Fawkes night.

With unaccustomed helpfulnesses we
Would cut back shrubs and overhanging tree,
We chopped down asters and the golden rod,
And runner beans with crisply ripened pod.

No nasty smelly rubber on our fires,
Before the days of mountains of old tyres;
The garden waste was saved for just that date,
For which our friends and family had to wait.

We did not find the need for food or drink,
Of ancient politics we did not think,
But made a Guy, though for him could not spare
Some proper clothes - our own we had to wear.

But still we had our hour of harmless joy,
Red-letter night for every girl and boy.
We each had sparklers in a ha'penny pack
And ran from naughty, scary, Jumping Jack.
Rotating Catherine wheels refused to turn
But somehow no one ended with a burn.
Our dad's set off the rockets to the sky
With starry bursts, a wondrous sight on high.
We hated bangers even in those years,
Though dreadful bangs were yet to fuel our fears.

Charlotte Clare

OF NO COLOUR

Bonfire night is round again
But no colour, just a bang
We'll maybe see a bright white?
The night sky not of bright light
When rockets go off in the air
Two seconds of brightness we see there.
Sparklers that one holds in the hand
Last a minute, not so grand.
Bonfire burns till first light
Unless we've rain, so put out might.

Michael D Bedford

IF ONLY
(And I'm called Bonnie)

If only tonight
It would pour with rain
So we wouldn't have
Dreadful fireworks *again!*
I was a happy Springer Spaniel
But my wits have just fled,
I'm shaking and puffing
And I've lost my street cred.
We've had bangers and rockets
For weeks every night
And my nice liver markings
Have now turned quite white.
I've asked all my friends
When I'm out on my walks
And they blame it all
On some chap - Guy Fawkes.
Well, he must be a nutter
And if he steps on my drive
I'll have his guts for garters
And not leave him alive.
I'm a most reasonable Springer,
But I've got to get tough,
For the sake of my sanity
Enough is enough!

Gloria Thorne

THE GREAT BONFIRE COLLECTING RITUAL

Bonfire night, tinder collecting
Always began in earnest,
From the 11th of October
For some unknown reason.
Pleading with our neighbours
To look in their sheds
And autumn littered back gardens,
For any suitable items to burn.
Dead dahlia stems, pruning from privets,
Old armchairs and rotten timber.
It was really quite difficult,
Since at the time,
There was still a wartime salvage collection.
From newspapers to rags, bones and old shoes,
I don't know where it all came from.
Much, if I remember correctly,
Was gale-broken branches and fallen leaves.
Long before composting was invented,
Piled up in old Arthur Payne's
Weedy and neglected back garden.
This sacred pyre had to be guarded,
As the neighbourhood children
In the late evening's lingering twilight
Were given to raiding and stealing.
Or even worse, most vindictively,
Like Viking marauders, setting it ablaze,
Seemingly hours before the great day.
When that happened it was terrible,
With much swearing and lamenting.
Back in those madcap, childhood days.

Jonathan Pegg

BONFIRE NIGHT

As Bonfire Night comes round again,
I'd like to make my feelings plain.

Fireworks and bonfires I deplore,
Guy Fawkes has a lot to answer for.

I find it really hard and try as I might -
I can't get excited about Bonfire Night.

Please don't think I'm being funny -
I believe it's such a waste of money.

To me it's just one big joke -
All that cash going up in smoke.

I know it only happens once a year,
But it clearly pollutes the atmosphere.

Before lighting a bonfire, hear my pleas,
Is there a hedgehog hiding in the leaves?

Up in the sky, the fireworks cascade,
It's a busy night for the Fire Brigade.

People have ignored the Firework Code,
So hospital casualties have overflowed.

Terrified animals jump out of their skin,
Responsible owners must keep pets in.

Only organised displays to be planned,
All other fireworks should be banned.

Rosemary Davies

NOVEMBER FIFTH

Gunpowder, treason and plot
November the fifth
forget us not.
The Houses of Parliament
blown sky high
if Guy Fawkes and plotters
hadn't been caught.
Build a bonfire great
with the Guy on top
exploding fireworks
that were legally bought.
Treason meant hanging, long ago,
the Houses of Parliament
will astound
the night Guy Fawkes
was abound.

Margery Rayson

All Because Of Guy Fawkes

Set bright against the eerie dark
Shapes dazzle as pure visions spark.
How many patterns can you see?
Effective with the naked eye
Looking upward - the painted sky
To behold splendour in majesty.

Massed lights aglow converge in dance
Cascading colours with sounds advance.
How many patterns can you see?
Sheer eloquence on display
In memory of this day.
We behold splendour in majesty.

Janet Collinson

GUY FAWKES

Out of the dark November night
A bonfire blazes, warm and bright.
Sparklers shed waterfalls of light,
While children's eyes shine with delight
And all because of Guy.

Some claim he was a spy,
'Gunpowder, treason and plot'
Shall never be forgotten,
As long as children like to play
And make the night as bright as day,
With fireworks lighting up the sky,
While bonfires burn a dummy Guy.

Don't get me wrong, I don't approve
The drastic way he would remove,
The building and the MP's too,
It was a wicked thing to do.
And yet . . . and yet . . . I don't know why
I feel I rather like this Guy!

Mary Hodges

BONFIRE NIGHT

I think
Of cowering
Under the stairs,
Saying no
To bonfire
Soup.
Turning away
The parkin.
Treacly though
It is;
I think of
Pouring cold
Water on
The Catherine
Wheels
Of sousing
Out the
Flames
Completely
With the
Garden hose;
But it is bonfire
Night and
I must tense
Up,
Put up my
Anorak hood
Around my
Ears and
Do none
Of those.

Janet M Baird

FIREWORK NIGHT

Look at the big rocket Mummy!
See how high it flies into the night sky.
Leaving burning fairy flowers,
Showering into the dark night.
Shimmering glory lights the dark.

Watch the Roman candle Daddy!
See it shoot and spark glittering stars.
Their fiery golden rain sprinkles the air,
Silver wriggles and bangs,
Colours of beauty abound.

Catherine wheel, oh Catherine wheel.
I love to see you spin.
Look at the magic fire
Circling around the pin.
Listening to the crystals as they hit the ground.

Oh look at the sad old guy,
He sits high on top of the fire, so grand.
Watch as he burns into the night sky,
His hat has toppled over,
But still he blazes on.

The Bonfire Night is nearly done.
But weren't the colours wonderful,
Lighting up the night sky like stars?
Thousands twinkling, spinning downward.
Didn't we have fun?

Jo Lodge

GUY FAWKES NIGHT

'Remember, remember the 5th of November,'
And we surely do as well
Because *we* dressed up as the Guy
And we all looked so swell.

We had our faces blackened
With soot from up the chimney,
Mending wool stuck under our nose
To make us look more trimly!

Long coats, and left-off battered hats
Upon our heads we wore
Then up and down Victoria Road
We went from door to door.

'A penny for the Guy?' we asked
But first we were inspected.
'No one could recognise these Guys'
That's what we suspected.

We'd share our pennies out at night
When the day was at an end,
And really felt quite wealthy
With what we had to spend.

But the real best time was at the end of the day
When in our backyard we went,
To light Catherine wheels, Sparklers, Jumping Jacks
And until all the Bangers were spent.

Guy Fawkes Night came late in year
But it was such fun.
From early morn 'till late at night
When all the day was done.

Mollie D Earl

THE FIFTH OF NOVEMBER
(Dedicated to Mum Stella)

She wasn't a guy, she was a girl
Born in nineteen hundred and five.
She was born in a house on Exmoor
Where she lived and worked and thrived.

Stella was our hardworking Mum
Who brought up us kids in the war.
It was scrubbing and polishing,
Cooking and shopping,
But always an open door.

Village life to me was different somehow,
To the town life, I'm used to now.
In days gone by it was doors open wide
Cakes on the baking tray side by side.

But leading up to November fifth
We made an old Guy to put on the sticks.
Old trousers! Old hat! And a pair of old shoes!
Stuffed out with old papers! Yesterday's news.

Nightfall we gathered, the village clan
Squibs going off and cakes in our hand
All eyes on the Guy, that funny old fella
And everyone saying, 'Happy Birthday, Stella!'

For November the fifth was Mum's special day
If there's stars in the sky I always say,
That's Mum with her sparklers
Just letting us know -
What fun we all had
All those years, long ago.

Rachel Mary Mills

BONFIRE BURNING

Fireworks, toffee apples, bonfires burning,
Safety first. Beware! Handle with care!
Turnip lanterns, children cheering.
Fireworks, toffee apples, bonfires burning.
Barbecue meat, slowly turning
Look to the sky, stand and stare.
Fireworks, toffee apples, bonfires burning,
Safety first. Beware! Handle with care!

Heather Denham

BONFIRE NIGHT

Remember, remember
The fifth of November
And so the saying goes.

Yes, it's that time of year
With fireworks, flares and bonfire glows.
As I gaze out of the window, bumps and bangs I hear
In the sky, the pretty sparkles of a rocket let off near.

I go back to my childhood with my brother, sisters and mates
As every Bonfire Night we would congregate
In our tiny garden to celebrate.
This Guy Fawkes night, oh they were the days!
Dad collected wooden boxes from work to build a bonfire high,
Whilst my brother and I made a Guy -
Using Granddad's old suit. Mother's nylons for a head
And Dad's flat cap, all stuffed with straw.
We wheeled him around in a rusty old pram
Calling out, 'Penny for the Guy!'
As we went from house to house, we did quite well
With shiny new pennies, threepenny bits and a sixpence or two.
We felt quite sad though when Dad placed our Guy on the top
Then watched him burn as Dad let the fireworks off.
In our woolly mittened hands, sparklers we had
Swirling them around, 'Not too close to your eyes,' warned Dad.
With Catherine wheels, rockets, bangers
Jumping Jacks which chased us around.
It was all very exciting and screams abound.
Mother placed potatoes upon the bonfire at the base,
Cooked in their jackets, loads of butter, delicious to taste.
Then when the fire dwindled, we watched the embers glow
Until it was time for bed and we had to go.
Now I am older, the magic of it all still my delight,
On this November the fifth, Bonfire Night.

Maggie Strong

Bonfire Night

An angel in disguise,
As a rocket caught a cherub
By surprise.
As we watched
Some more got matched
And Guy Fawke's bum
Is a glowing merchandise.

There is a beacon on yer hill
It's our Guy sending signals.
Would a lighthouse be a match?
No save yer money, for another patch.
It's funny how you smile
Because I have never seen a spectrum
So nice and beautiful.

Hardeep

BONFIRE NIGHT

I remember another Bonfire Night,
the year 1945, the end of World War II.
We built a huge bonfire; the first one
many of us; born in the late 1930's had seen.
There hadn't been bonfires or fireworks
during the war.

The fire burned brightly and people reminisced,
there was the fragrance of burning wood;
Yellow and orange flames danced above us.
The fireworks were loud and clear.

Yet our thoughts went beyond the fires that
had burned our blitzed cities.
Our thoughts went back almost 350 years
to that first bonfire, burning effigies of
Guy Fawkes.

What would that night have been like?
And then back to the present day - and
Mother calling, 'Supper is ready!'
And we enjoyed the appetising taste of
beautiful hot food and potatoes cooked
in the fire.

Janet Cavill

THE TIME OF YEAR AGAIN!

Night skies are once again - a blaze of colour before our eyes
Young ones call out with joy - as they dance around a fire bright.
What can it mean - why all the fuss - what is it all about?
It is to remember that a man by the name of Sir Guy Fawkes
Had big ideas and tried to blow up the Houses of Parliament -
As a result, we have been having fun every fifth of November
                                                    ever since.

Rowland Patrick Scannell

THE 5TH OF NOVEMBER

I remember, I remember those earlier Novembers
Which held a special magic - just for me!
In retrospect, I see again the cheerful glowing embers
Of the 'bonfire-in-the-garden' after tea.

I recall the mute appeal of each spinning Catherine wheel
And the 'flare-path' made by rockets in the skies.
It's easy to reveal - just how little children feel -
With reflected light from 'Sparklers' in their eyes.

Such colour and such noise - enjoyed by girls and boys -
Immortalised by Guy Fawkes and his plot.
For those elusive joys they would sacrifice their toys -
Just like 'the boy that Santa Claus forgot!'

But one more family member - I ask you to remember,
Is the child who lit a 'bomb' then fell asleep!
He never woke again; he was *mine* and *I* remember.
I remember, I remember . . . and I weep!

Maureen Sponar

MAGICAL LIGHTS

As the spray of light reached the sky
It was such a sight! I tell no lie!
Such heat as I stood by the blaze
My surroundings fill with a magical haze.

The little man at the top of the pile
Was so life-like, it made me smile?
As the families gathered all around
All were mesmerised by each new sound.

See the look on the little boy's face
As his dad puts the firework in place.
With the fuse lit, the child looked aghast
Drawing a breath at the sudden blast.

Magical lights filled the blackened skies
As the rocket takes flight to the air it flies
Tiny drops of sparkling light
Trickling down on this enchanting night.

All but some were having a ball,
The dogs and cats didn't like it all!
They cowered in fear and ran away
Not understanding it was only play!

Bonfire Night is a day to remember
Every year on the 5th of November.
The lights, the aromas and the sounds
Constantly thrill us in leaps and bounds.

Some memories of this day can bring sadness
The pleasures can turn the day to madness.
Fireworks can be dangerous to fools
Don't be a victim and remember the rules!

Rose Murdoch

REMEMBER, REMEMBER

Rockets whoosh in the sky
Each one it climbs like seven
Fizzing the dark, like soda-pop
In a pyrotechnic heaven.

Bangers thrown by mittened hands
The children shriek in fright
Coloured fountain's rainbows play
Kaleidoscope the night.

Catherine's wheel, twist-twirls around
With its tail aflame
A martyr she for Christians sake
Remembered by this game.

Old Guy sits gloomy 'top of the fire
His welfare quite unheeded.
With the Parliament we have today
I wish he had succeeded!

Sarah Blackmore

REMEMBER, REMEMBER

'Guy Fawkes night's late in Windsor, no wait,
'sno bonfire, it's the castle which blazes
Bet there'll be a few late 'fireworks' crackling
and spluttering in the Commons.
Look, there's Her Majesty, see how she solemnly gazes
At burning timber and melting stained-glass
in anorak and Wellingtons.

And there look, a human chain commanded by
the Duke of York - Andrew.
While above, on hydraulic platforms, fireman
onto flames are hoses playing.
As along the chain pass prayer book, chalice,
plaque, carved pew.
Vase, candlestick, embroidered kneeling-cushions
and oil painting.

Through the night, firemen toil to prevent
a catastrophe
In castle from where the Queen sends
Christmas salutations.
Comes the dawn and MI5 disguised as Fire Chiefs
search for charred papers linking Edward VIII to Reich *Nazi*.
And in the press and media, news of a Trojan horse
from the Duke of Edinburgh . . .
Her Majesty's home belongs to the nation.

A Greek gift; the good old British taxpayer*
will foot the restoration bill,
No matter that there's high unemployment, recession
and rumblings for royal equivalent of 'perestroika'.
And relations between the 'firm' and populace
are taking on a chill,

But what's this one hears from Prince Edward?
'Let's challenge Anneka!'

*   before our tax evading Queen became a tax payer 'voluntarily' and couldn't afford the fire insurance premium!

R Wiltshire

FIGURE ON THE FIRE

Fan the flames,
let history explain,
the colours, the shapes,
the whistles and the games.

The Guy on the bonfire
says November the 5th
and his words are rockets
in the air.

Brocks, barbecues, blues and be gone,
Fawkes for the fireworks, let his legend live on.
Shooting stars from a box
light up the sky
and the sparklers are signs in the dark.

Gunpowder girls
strike matches alight,
and in the heat of the moment
and a mouthful of sticks,
the figure is burning,
his last words are lost.

And the world is on fire again.

M C Jones

Guy Fawkes

On the fire, rockets go higher and higher
I watch the flames from the bonfire
Starburst explodes in the sky
Colours like stars
The smell of gunpowder hangs in the air
Pyramids shoot balls of fire
Colours change as they get higher
Higher and higher
Guy Fawkes sits on the top of the fire
November the 5th is here
Never return to a firework once it's out
Always take care if in doubt
Always follow the firework code
November the 5th should be safe
It should not be forgotten for a reason -
Guy Fawkes was hung for treason!

S L Groves

Rockets, Smoke And Glitter

'Penny for the guy,
Penny for the guy,'
Out on the streets,
The children did cry.
They'd dressed him in old hat, jacket and trousers,
Stuffed with rags,
With hands, feet and face,
Made of paper bags,
To be burned on the bonfire,
This was Guy
On firework night,
He would die!

Fireworks sizzling,
Boom! Voom! Zoom!
See them soaring,
Bing! Bang! Boom!
Catherine wheels,
Spin round and round,
Whizz! Fizz! Sizz!
Is the sound.
Jumping Jacks,
Are they banned?
And silver fairy sparklers,
To hold in the hand.
Bonfires flaming,
Make a lingering haze of grey,
The aroma hanging on the air,
To the very next day.
Rockets, smoke and glitter,
Red, yellow, white.
Blue, purple and green,
Crackling light.

Children's eyes,
Light up with thrill,
To see the colours,
Explode and spill.
The 5th of November,
Crash! Bang! Hooray!
For the beautiful,
Firework display.

Carol Ann Darling

MASTERS OF THE SKY

November 5th: I watch the city down below
as fireworks crackle like machine guns
and it's as if the flickering neon city lights
are ascending into the smoke-filled night
and exploding into a rainbow of colours
outshining the stars and moon
peering jealously from far above.

Yet this glory is as transient as human life,
a second's lustre then lost forever.
Animals cower as children stare in awe,
screeching sounds like a Stalin organ
racing across the sky like a shooting star.
It's late: a rogue firework screams up high,
the stars and moon again, masters of the sky.

Guy Fletcher

SURPLUS

Can't stop, got a backlog of imagination to shift.
Up to my ears in surplus ideas
Induced by sensory deprivation
Or two weeks' nights to you.

Morning, after twelve hours catch-up.
Scything through wet grass,
Pegging out smalls in carpet-worn slippers.
Background sights, new delights.
Every child a poem,
Every pensioner a central character in a play entitled
'Social Assassin'

Last night, bonfires blazed
While rockets dizzied the stars.
Today, all is grey and forgotten.
A child that kicks at a charred Guy
And slits open the spent skin
Of a Roman candle
Is really the murderer in my eyes.

Simon Daniels

A Real Bonfire

A Sparkler, a rocket, some bangers
Were kept safe inside old aircraft hangers
But a spark went astray
Turning night into day
And we went to the moon with the Clangers!

Maureen Westwood O'Hara

NOVEMBER 5TH

The bangs deafening, flames flicker and dance,
The night sky aglow with an orange light,
Around the bonfire, happy children prance,
Showers of golden rain fall through this night.
Guy Fawkes sits aloft on his burning throne,
The crackling embers glow red beneath him,
Hand-held sparklers make patterns of their own,
Dazzling fireworks transform a night once dim.

November the sixth dawns cold and dreary,
Debris scattered, firework tubes damp and dead,
Once bright sparkler wands left black and wiry,
Charred embers cindery, no longer red.
Last night, explosive excitement resounds,
Today, a dark sooty patch marks the ground!

Pat Heppel

BONFIRE NIGHT SONNET

Flash! Bang! Crackle! Whoosh! Blam!
It sounds just like a 'Batman' TV script.
The bloody nuisances don't give a damn,
All the relentless noise gives you the pip:
Animals are frightened by the noise,
They all run and try to hide away.
From sick, sadistic evil girls and boys,
Who view scaring of pets as simple play:
Considerable expense goes up in smoke,
Whilst everybody moans of being skint.
Who buys these fireworks if they're all broke?
They must have cost some silly sod a mint!
But if November 5th's where they belong,
How come the nuisance lasts so bloody long?

Mick Nash

NOVEMBER

Fruits . . . fog . . . and fireworks -
November's omens.
Fauna finding autumn's fruits
in winter preparation.
Fog-enfolding day's half-light
in the weakening sun.

Fawkes-focussed
families flame the fires:
and with wide-eyed wonder
watch as fireworks explode
in fizzing incandescence
in the November darkness.

Joy Morton

JUBILEE BONFIRE

Sun sinks and in evening's chill we wait,
No summer warmth to cheer these revellings.
And was it thus when once the watchers stood
On lonely hilltops lest Armada come?
Less grim our purpose, no fear as we stand,
This fire, no beacon of impending doom.
And then the first flame flickers, fire is lit,
And all at once the night becomes alive.
Upwards the sparks fly, carrying our thoughts
Towards the stars. Eyes light, flames roar,
And suddenly our bodies warm in the festive air.
Then song, as loving hearts uplift to celebrate.
Now embers glow and in the midnight voices fade,
Clouds part and comes the moon as if to join
Our gathering, and we have kept Jubilee together.

Christopher T Coney

BONFIRE NIGHT

A magical time when I was a child,
It seemed as though the world went wild!
A bonfire in the field at the bottom of our street,
Kids collected fireworks, Mums made things to eat.
Everyone got together to share this magic night,
Overawed with 'oohs' and 'aahs'. Enchanted at the sight!
Today it's so expensive and like a field of war,
Explosions, ever louder, they shake you to the core!
I think it's time for changes, each town with one display!
Organised by the Fire Brigade. Safety, the order of the day.
It was the highlight of the year. Long ago in my youth,
Now it's getting out of control, people acting so uncouth!
It would be oh so sad, to ban it altogether.
How I loved it in a gentler age, however cold, the weather.
Sparklers, fountains, Catherine wheels, rockets in a bottle.
Now it's too much like bombs going off, full throttle.
Screams and whistles rend the sky in gigantic explosion,
Colour streams across the night in a succession of confusion.
Every year, people get burned or badly injured,
My dog fell downstairs in fright at a banger thro' the door,
Broke her back, died in agony.
I don't like fireworks any more!

E M Eagle

Bonfire Night Memories Revisited

On Bonfire Night as I watched my grandchildren's faces,
My mind suddenly leapt to other times and places.
When I was their age, our pleasures were cheaper,
But then again, modern pockets seem so much deeper.

For weeks before hand we'd be scouring the local wood,
Scrounging and salvaging anything that was any good.
Knocking on neighbours' doors for anything that burned,
Promising them a prominent position in return.

We stored it in outhouses, in neat little piles,
Looking at each other with secretive smiles.
As the time drew nearer we got so afraid,
That the other local gangs would make a raid.

Mother would be making toffee and apples on sticks,
There'd be parkin, pie and peas then we'd be sick.
We soon brightened up when the fireworks began,
Then the fire was lit to burn our replica Guy Fawkes man.

Like everything else, today it's all commercialised,
No room for the small man, no more free enterprise.
Community fires and organised firework display,
The Council makes sure that everyone pays.

D I Muncaster

BONFIRE NIGHT

On Bonfire Night the flames lick high
Into the dark November sky.
Children's eyes shining bright
As the fireworks light the night.
Sparklers crackling, spitting stars,
Rockets shooting
Heading for Mars!
Bursts of colour explode in the air
Glowing flowers everywhere.
Whooshing, whistling
Banging, fizzing!
Oohs from the crowd
As something goes whizzing.
In the frosty night everyone's muffled
In hats and scarves
And gloves and duffles.
Steaming soup is ready at last
Bangers and tatties for the repast!
Warm and happy
The kids say goodnight.
Dogs and cats get over their fright
Now all is calm -
They stretch and yawn,
Curl up to sleep until the morn'!

Anne Lawry

BONFIRE NIGHT FIREWORKS

The fifth of November
It's only one day
But it's carried on for weeks
I am sorry to say.

We all like the fun
And all the coloured lights
Fireworks also give
Many people frights.

Like everything else
Things get out of hand
Which a lot of young people
Just don't understand.

Animals take fright
When not kept inside
Even organised fireworks
Need adults to guide.

Rules should be made
Fireworks before ten
The very young and aged
Will not be awakened then.

November the fifth
The one and only day
Guy Fawkes tried to blow up Parliament
Let's keep it that way.

Explosions are heard
Night after night
If we keep the anniversary
Let's get it right.

Violetta J Ferguson

MOMENTS OF LIGHT

They start around the end of October
Then it's stop, start, stop, start
Up to the middle of November
They are beautiful and the colours are wow!

Shooting high into the sky
Green, red, purple, gold stars that fly
Rockets that take your breath away
Dream what they will show in that next moment.

Whoosh! Bang! Crackle! Crackle!
Lighting up the sky just for a short time
Sparkles that sparkle in the night
Laughter on the evening breeze - Ahh!

Fireworks on the 5th November.

Carole A Cleverdon

GUNPOWDER PLOT
(In the year of Our Lord 1605)

Gunpowder, gunpowder,
We blow them sky high,
Within the darkened cellar of Parliament
Came the biggest plot.

A conspiracy, so seasoned with contempt,
With sedition and treason may the Catholics rot.
On the 5th of November, they were surprised,
By the king's secret procedures and guize.

Who discovered the Gunpowder Plot in time?
Oh Parliament! Oh Parliament!
Came so close to being blown apart
With the rebels deliberate, wicked plot.

Who sympathised for the Catholic cause,
To overthrow King James 1 and his laws?
Whilst plotting for weeks in an ale house in London town,
On the 5th of November, we never forget!

A treasonable, dastardly, cunning deed,
By the Catholic plotters, who wished
King James 1 and his Parliament dead
For Guy Fawkes and his fellow conspirators who fled.

Are but traitors, not martyrs,
On the eve of November 5th, 1605
Inconceivable was their aim and goal,
To bring total destruction to Parliament's Hall of Fame

Whilst inciting the Gunpowder Plot
With insurrection and rebellion as their game.

Gunpowder, gunpowder,
We blow them sky high,
Within the darkened cellar of Parliament,
Came the biggest plot.

James Stephen Cameron

GUY FAWKES NIGHT

When I was a child
Guy Fawkes night was exciting.
The prospect of flashes
Colourful and bright,
Had us on tenterhooks weeks before.
On that night, we gathered around
A fire so cheerful, sparklers in hand.
Excitement mounted as flames soared,
Catherine wheels whirred
As Jumping Jacks leapt.
Golden rain, Roman candles,
Rockets that whizzed.
Lit up the sky, red, green and gold,
Blue, white and silver,
Were seen in abundance.
Not many people minded the bangs
They weren't that fearful,
Shocking or loud
And lasted only one night.
Now we have booms,
Loud and deafening
Assailing the senses,
Reawakening memories
Both painful and sad.
How I long for yesteryear,
When Guy Fawkes was fun
And came once a year.

Therese G Gilbert

THE FIREWORK PARTY

Two boys agonise over their choice.
Long hours deciding the fireworks
to purchase for bonfire night.
A place for old favourites, certainly!
The newly introduced, untried,
a more grudging purchase.

Collections gloated over by small boys
like Scrooge with his money bags.
Boxes laid carefully on beds
for close inspection and approval.
Rivals admire or condemn selections
with comments on sad omissions.

The new coloured matches blaze
with flame of bright red or green
mesmerise and, unnoticed nears its end,
burns the boy's finger and is dropped into the box!
Wild panic as the match lights a Roman candle
whose touch paper will not be extinguished.

The Roman candle, now aflame, is a signal
for rockets, Catherine wheels, jumping Jacks
and strings of bangers to take their turn
to terrorise the young seeking sanctuary under a bed.
Not before time, an adult rescues them
from their smoke filled, smouldering retreat.

Guy Fawkes day arrives and, once more
Fawkes and his friend Catesby are imprisoned,
but this time before the event and under house arrest.

Robert Allen

REMEMBER THE 5TH OF NOVEMBER

Remember; remember the 5th of November,
As rockets light up the sky.
Remember; remember the 5th of November,
As the sirens go rushing by.
'Oh look at the jumping Jack flash,'
As the hospital swing behind with a crash.
'Oh look the Catherine wheel's going round and round,'
While the operating pumps make a mournful sound.
The banger explodes in the cold night sky,
While in the draughty corridor the family cry.
'Wow there goes a whiza, look at it spin,'
Poor Mom can barely contain the pain she's in.
The Roman candle bursts to life in the sky,
The surgeon sadly reports, 'She'll lose the sight of her eye.'
The night is nearly over, the fireworks almost gone,
But for one small child the nightmare will live on.
The fireworks are almost done now, put away for another year,
But the danger still lingered, the aftermath ever near.
And the toddler holds a sparkler in her tiny-gloved fist,
While almost unknowing Mom holds tightly to her wrist.
And somewhere a little girl stares with only one eye,
Her parents offer up a prayer, 'Dear God, *Why?*'

Lynne Cassels

BONFIRE

Bonfire, bonfire, it's a beautiful sight,
Bang! Whizz! Crack go the fireworks at night.

The rockets are exploding
While the others are loading.

They light up the night,
They're very bright.

You can't stop the noise,
Bonfire, bonfire, bright with the light.

Lucy May Harrison (9)

BONFIRE NIGHT

Bonfire, bonfire, glitters and grows
Raging fires that the wind will blow
Then the fire shows
Then you get numb toes.
Then the fire goes quite low
When it's finished, you go!

Holly Laisby & Beth Pedley (9)

BONFIRE NIGHT

Bonfire, bonfire it's a beautiful sight
Bang, whiz, crack go the fireworks at night.
Bonfire, bonfire lights up the dark
When they let rip, they make it spark.
Bonfire, bonfire the fireworks are exploding,
While the other ones are lighting and loading.

Rebecca Smith & Lucy Harrison (9)

FIREWORK NIGHTS

The first of October
Twelve-o-one am
There's the first bang
It's that time again!
From now till December
Each and very night
There'll be bangs and flashes
You see if I'm right!
Who is it who sells them
So early in the year?
They must know they'll only
Bring us terror and fear!
And those young lads
Throwing bangers in the street
At passing cars and buses
Think they're really neat!
The poor old family dog
Who's steady as a rock
Now turned to jelly
Shaking in its socks!
We all love fireworks
The colours and the lights
So let's stick to spectaculars
And Bournemouth Pier on Friday nights!

Rowena

FIREWORKS - TWO VIEWS
(For my grandson, Warren, aged 18 months)

To delighted sighs and screams,
Long gold and silver streams,
With booms and bangs and whines,
Blossomed above into huge coloured dandelions.

The shiny balls then changed again,
Breaking into umbrellas of crackling rain,
Falling over upturned faces and heads,
Droplets of greens, blues and reds.

But, one little boy
Certainly didn't enjoy
The show of pretty aerial flowers,
Exploding into noisy showers.

He didn't like the sight
Of the dazzling light
And the sounds hurt his ears -
It all brought him to tears.

Maybe, when he's older -
A little bolder -
He won't have to bury his baby head
On Mum's shoulder, in such innocent dread.

Joan Howlett

Fireworks On The Fifth

The secular, the scheming globe revolves
from one dank, dismal
winter to the next;
disastrous wars ensue,
the firmament stays blue,
eggshell, indigo and royal hue.
Homo-Sapiens vexed,
sees no great miracle earth's problem solves;
then children chirrup, 'Penny for the Guy!'
Tired eyes forget, gaze upwards at the sky.
November night is numb,
vast the heaven's arc
and black, then fireworks come,
ravishing the dark;
no human voice resounds from outer space,
no blessing honeys man's profound disgrace,
yet futile aspirations join the race,
aiming inhibition at a height,
damning disappointment this one night.
Crimson, purple, amber, all mean love,
rocketing reminders soar above,
defiance penetrates the gloom;
though clangour cries of earthly doom
ripe colour murderous, supreme,
contrives to manifest a dream.
All year our supplications drone,
their pathos keen, austere, alone.
Now poised, explosive ploys no patience brook;
our whims ignite, enthral, then bid us look.

Ruth Daviat

Enlightening

The night belies the next half an hour,
Cold and silence belying the dormant power,
Then suddenly the crackle of the Catherine wheel,
And the rockets deafeningly retched squeal.
Catch you off guard and with jolted surprise,
With the air filling with impressed sighs,
Bright colours including red, green and gold,
Such beautiful explosions to behold,
Resonating in the sky, deep dark blue,
Illuminating everything near into our view,
In the morning you have to laugh at your self-inflicted joke,
You've literally watched £80 go up in smoke!

Mark Redfern

GUNPOWDER TREASON

Remember, remember the fifth of November,
Gunpowder, treason and plot;
A failed attempt the Protestant faith to pre-empt,
By getting rid of the King, a Scot.

But somebody thought it was better to send a stern letter
To one of the peers, warning him not to show up
To that evening's oration on affairs of the nation,
As the place was about to blow up.

The peer, all officious, thought, *this is suspicious,*
Whoever this is has some gall
To be so malicious to do mass murder so vicious,
I do not like this at all!

So he laid down his cards and called out the guards
To rip out this deed by the roots.
They searched high and low, until, way down below,
They found at least seven scheming brutes.

There was gunpowder galore covering most of the floor -
They'd been planning this for over a year!
Some were killed on sight as they tried to take flight,
While Guy Fawkes was dragged out by the ear.

They gave him such a hard time, he admitted the crime,
Including a full list of names
From the first to the last in the attempt to blast
Into eternity good King James.

But if he had any hope of avoiding the rope
By grassing up on his mates,
That hope was soon wrecked as he hung by the neck
And swung by the Traitors' Gate.

So lest you forget and agree to abet
Another such crime so immense,
Remember, remember the fifth of November,
For treason still is a hanging offence!

Kathy Rawstron

NOVEMBER FIFTH

Goodbye, goodbye to bonfire night
Let's get rid of this annual fright,
Now the time has come to quit
I hate it, I hate it, I hate it.

Every year my attitude hardens
To explosions in the gardens
And eruptions in the streets
As at being loudest each competes

Shaking buildings, rattling bins
Making us jump out of our skins
Poor old dogs bark and cower
Children feel the destructive power

People burned and scarred forever
Firework throwing isn't clever.
'Gunpowder, treason and plot'
Terrorist threat must not be forgot

I love an organised firework display
A blazing fire, even the effigy can stay
Toffee apples, hot dogs, parkin and soup
The pleasure of socialising in a group

Let's keep bonfire 'night' but what a joke
There's a month of bangs and smoke
Issue firework licences and remember
Bonfire night is only on 5th November.

P S D MacArthur

BONFIRE NIGHT - PAST AND PRESENT MEMORIES

Remember, remember the 5th of November,
Is the rhyme that we learned at school.
To keep far away from the dangerous spray,
In my day was trendy and cool.
There were Catherine wheels, Roman candles,
Traffic light and fairy fountains,
With rockets and jumping Jacks too.
We'd have jacket tatties roasted on the fire,
With mushy peas, mint sauce and stew.
There would also be parkin and treacle toffee,
Home-made by my mother and me.
We'd start when it got really dark,
And so the dogs for too long didn't bark,
We'd finish about eight-thirty at night,
Our neighbours enjoying the fun and delight.

Now it's much different from what I remember,
When bonfire night was the 5th of November.
The loud bangs, booms, bright flashes that never end,
Is enough to drive everyone right round the bend.
This scares the animals, giving them a fright,
They cannot stand the noise, night after night.
People who work don't get enough sleep.
They are not able themselves in good health to keep.
Older people relate it to being in a war zone,
The council are trying to get something done.
My wish is not to be a miserly killjoy,
But to continue with something everyone can enjoy.
To keep the noise down with a cut-off time,
I'm sure would suit most people really fine.

Janet Ramsden

Pleased To Remember The Fifth Of November

Guy Fawkes night comes round again
And we are praying it won't rain.
We hope the tickets haven't all been sold
As we wrap up well against the cold.
Setting out in the car to Moss End
Parents, kids, grans or just a friend.
The bonfire is well alight
Brightening and warming the chilly night.
We're greeted by torch light in the dark
And are shown exactly where to park.

The mud is thick because of rain
Will we ever get out again?
We are assured if we get stuck
We'll be pulled free by a truck.
The fields have been strewn with straw and hay
Across which we make our way.
Towards the fairy lights of the fair
Press on all, we'll soon be there.
Roundabout rides, tombola and a hot dog stall
Candyfloss and ice cream, a choice for all.

With everyone fed and feeling OK
We are ready to view the firework display.
Bangs and whooshes and rockets so high
Sending stars and patterns across the sky.
A good half hour of 'oohs' and 'aahs',
Then we make our way back to our cars.
Marshalled out and on our way
To enjoy a cuppa to end the day.
Thanks Bracknell Forest Council for this show
If repeated next year we are sure to go.

Enid Thomas

BONFIRE NIGHT

Bonfire night
What a sight
Children's faces filled with delight
All lit up with an orange glow
As the flickering flames leap and grow
Now every eye is raised to the sky
To see the rockets explode with lights
And then slowly die.

B J Green

THOUGH NOVEMBER SKIES ARE SOMETIMES RED AND GLOWING: (I REMEMBER, REMEMBER SUMMER WHEN EVERYTHING IS SHOWING!) - WITH SWEET LOVE FLOWING!

Riding on my nut-brown pony towards the closing of a cold November the Fifth day;
I saw the blood-red sunset and wondered at such exquisite exhilerating glory as we wended our cold yet happy way.
Though I'm only eighteen summers old, I'm a true teenage woman with urgent needs and deeds to do of my own;
As I looked up at the awesome beauty, I trembled as I shivered and dreamed the ethereal sight was for me alone.
Oh how I longed for the warm sultry days of heavenly summer, now just a happy memory fair
When the sun seemed to shine for ever and I could cast off the robes of inhibition and swim totally naked without a care.
Or dress in the latest summer fashion showing off my sexy bare belly line:
With matching pierced dimpled navel complete with jewel and dangling chain, titillating and divine.
I like to show a full bare nine inches tantalising below the voluptuous hip!
And although I don't often go topless, I'm not shy when I dip.
For in the wine and dine days of full summer, I never have a care:
I'm an eighteen-year-old girlie-whirlie and take care of what I wear.
My mum told me she used to wear skinny bikinis and often went sweetly topless and bravely nude too,
She also liked to wear bell-bottom jeans with bells at the bottom to add to the trendy, appealing and well revealing bare hipster view!
Though she's my mum, I've got her into being well pierced and sexily tattooed daringly everywhere:
Well, she's only thirty-eight and doesn't like to be called square!
I have a tattoo of a laughing clown just above my teenaged navel, sweet and fair,

And my mum went one better and had one below her bounteous belly button of a rampant lion just for the dare.
In summer my mum goes happily crazy and we often exchange our own fashion gear for bare as much as we dare fun.

She puts on my razzle dazzle bouncing free boob tube, and wears a micro mini slung bare flesh low and raised high in the sun;
She just doesn't care and wears just a slip of a thong so she can show her glowing peach of a radiant bum,
While I wear her five inch stilettos, stockings, sussies and French frilly knickers with matching low-cut and backless ball gown;
We really do look a hedonistic swinging fab pair when we're
out on the town.
So I really do long for summer red-hot sunsets, when winter's cruel frost begins to bite deep and cruel;
And much as I like riding my nut-brown pony in winter, I'm not a fool. Though I can still dress up trendily and go out bopping with my mum to clubs and that,
Nothing can compare to the rosy-red summer when sometimes I ride nude and wearing nothing but flowers in my sunny hat.

Jackie J Docherty

EMBERS OF THE PAST

Cacophony of explosions shatter the night's stillness
like an array of Scud missiles homing in on their target,
Followed by a myriad blaze of colourful light of untold exotic intensity
Rupturing the ebony velvet of the night sky's fabric,
Reminding us that Bonfire Night is upon us once again.
Raising our childhood spectres through adult eyes as we now watch
this awesome spectacle with a new generation.
The appetising aroma of various hot food from piping hot jacket
potatoes leaving a steamy trail of seafaring galleons wafting in
                                                               the still air,
To sizzling sausages bathed in mustard in hot dogs tempting the
                                                                 saliva glands.
To the tantalising oaken, musky fragrance of burning wood,
Simultaneously mesmerising and warming us with their crackling
golden and amber flames from the soul-warming fires,
Dancing and reaching upwards to the protective penumbra of the
laser-light-like fireworks cascading overhead.
In-between, huge bonfires with effigies of hirsute Cavalier Guy
                                                          Fawkes on top, burn,
Reminding us that nearly four hundred years ago,
That ready warmonger, Religion, in the name of Catholicism
tried to incinerate both Protestant, Monarch and Parliament.
Treacherous traitors trying to forcibly transcribe their mode of
                                                       thinking and living,
Or martyrs fighting for a just cause?
Let the spectator decide, but never forget the blood-soaked reason
                                                    behind the celebration,
Lest history forget!

Robin Halder

BONFIRE NIGHT

Remember, remember,
Fifth of November,
A special occasion,
A traditional celebration,
With burning of Guy Fawkes' effigies,
And no sincere apologies,
Fireworks exploding,
Flames leaping,
Lighting of the sky,
Fragrance of burning so high,
All types of effects,
In the sky reflects,
All colours and hues,
All the time you choose.

Ramandeep Kaur (15)

Autumn Magic

Misty mornings, heavy with dew,
Lacy cobwebs with the sun shining through,
A cat's recent pawprints marking the grass,
An old black crow flapping lazily past.

Leaves on the trees turning red, gold and brown,
Until, like confetti, they float to the ground.
Children, with laughter echoing round,
Scuff through the leaves - a dry, crunching sound.

Bushes with berries, bejewelled red and black;
Squirrels hunting nuts for their winter stack.
Ah, smell the aroma of leaf and wood smoke
From bonfires that gardeners tend and stoke.

Smoky spirals climb to the skies
Where buzzards circle. Their keening cries
Pierce the stillness of the morning air,
Fieldmice scurry to hide in their lair.

Deer step daintily through the trees,
While stags fight rivals 'til loser flees.
The victor bellows, then gathers its herds.
The forest falls silent, except for the birds.

Harvests are gathered, abundant the yields.
Fieldfare and redwings flock to the fields.
The summer was tranquil. Now autumn is mellow.
Soon winter will come, with a roar and a bellow.

Gwen Hoskins

Autumn... Is It Good Or Bad?

A gentle breeze stirring in the air . . .
A cold wind whirling around me,
Trying to drag me off my feet,
Attempting to snatch away my warm, woollen coat.

Emerald green grass below my feet . . .
A carpet of leaves,
Crunching loudly with every step I take,
Yet they are so colourful.

Pretty and fragrant flowers in full bloom . . .
Petals spread all over the ground,
Flower heads in tatters,
No more sweet-smelling blossoms.

But . . . what about the good things about autumn?

Children dancing merrily around a bonfire,
Fireworks shooting into the sky like rockets,
Sparklers glittering in every hand,
A warm fire to warm up our cold hands and faces.

Hallowe'en pumpkins outside houses,
Trick and treaters all dressed up,
Pendle Hill is the place to be,
That is . . . if you are brave enough!

All that remains to ask is:

Autumn . . . good or bad?

Mrinalini Dey (12)

Fireworks

They raise like sudden fiery flowers,
They burst upon the night,
They fall to earth like burning showers
Of crimson, blue or white.

Like buds too wonderful to name,
Each miracle unfolds,
The Catherine wheel begins to flame
Like whirling marigolds.

Rockets and Roman candles make
An orchard in the sky,
Whence magic trees their petals shake,
Upon each gazing eye.

David Sheasby

ANCHOR BOOKS SUBMISSIONS INVITED
SOMETHING FOR EVERYONE

ANCHOR BOOKS GEN - Any subject, light-hearted clean fun, nothing unprintable please.

THE OPPOSITE SEX - Have your say on the opposite gender. Do they drive you mad or can we co-exist in harmony?

THE NATURAL WORLD - Are we destroying the world around us? What should we do to preserve the beauty and the future of our planet - you decide!

All poems no longer than 30 lines.
Always welcome! No fee!
Plus cash prizes to be won!

Mark your envelope (eg *The Natural World*)
And send to:
Anchor Books
Remus House, Coltsfoot Drive
Peterborough, PE2 9JX

OVER £10,000 IN POETRY PRIZES TO BE WON!

Send an SAE for details on our latest competition!